AMERICA GOES TO WAR

THE WAR ON TERROR

TIMELINES, FACTS, AND BATTLES

By Craig Boutland

ROSEN PUBLISHING

Published in 2023 by The Rosen Publishing Group, Inc.
2544 Clinton Street, Buffalo, NY 14224

Editor: Lindsey Lowe
Children's Publisher: Anne O'Daly
Design Manager: Keith Davis
Picture Manager: Sophie Mortimer

Picture Credits:
Front Cover: U.S. Department of Defense
Key: t = top, b = bottom, c = center
Adam Reynolds Photography: 47; AGP: Antoine Gyodri 29b; Alamy: Matteo Omied 7, PA Images 28, REUTERS 6, 17, 25b, 34, 40, 42, 55, 58, RGB Ventures 15, UPI 61b, ZUMA Press 53; EPA: Badri Media 23, Carlos Dias 25t, Akhtar Gulfam 35, Abed al Hafiz 49, Nabil Mounzer 46, Andy Rain 31, Spiegel.de 43, Abi Weda 9t; John Stanmeyer/VII: 52; Mark Peterson Photography: 8; Photoshelter: Mark Whittaker 18; Public Domain: 38-39, 39c, 39b, btselem 10-11, Paco Campus 30, CEE_HOPE Nigeria 26-27, Mstyslav Chernov 33c, Disaster and Emergency Management Presidency Turkey 61t, Mikhail Evstafiev 11c, Flickr/AMISOM 26, Bernard Gagnon 45t, Muhammad Ghafari 51t, Khairulash 10, Anne Knight 27c, Tomasz Kozlowski 32-33, www.kremlin.ru 51b, lemonade.fr 33t, Mil.ru 50-51b, Mona 50c, Qasioun News Agency 50t, sa.vakilian/mrostam 39t, Francois Schnell 11t, Zoheir Seidanloo 38, Shamsnn 50-51c, Tasnim News Agency/Milad Hamadi 60-61c, Times of India Handout 37t, Andreas Tojak 32, VOA 27t, VOA/Mahmoud Bali 44-45b; Ramin Talaie Photography: 59t; REUTERS: Romeo Ranoco 54t; Rick Ergenbright Photography: 36; Shutterstock: Alan Freed 9b, Amanda Haddox 14, Paolo Omero 15, Lizette Potgieter 13; United States Government: Department of Defense 16, 24, 44t, 44-45c, 54b, 57, Department of State 21t, 21c, U.S. Army 22, 44c, U.S. Army/Michael J. Nelson 29t, U.S. Marines/Staff Sgt Victor Mancillan 20-21, 60-61b, USAF/Air Mobility Command Public Affairs 60, White House 20; Xinhua Press: Wang Ye 37b; ZUMA Press: Minneapolis Star 59b, Toronto Star 56.

Cataloging-in-Publication Data

Names: Boutland, Craig.
Title: The War on Terror: timelines, facts, and battles / Craig Boutland.
Description: New York : Rosen Publishing, 2023. | Series: America goes to war| Includes bibliographic references, index and glossary.
Identifiers: ISBN 9781499473919 (pbk) | ISBN 9781499473926 (library bound) | ISBN 9781499473933 (ebook)
Subjects: LCSH: Afghan War, 2001- —Juvenile literature | Iraq War, 2003-2011— Juvenile literature | War on Terrorism, 2001-2009— Juvenile literature
Classification: LCC HV6432 B68 2023 | DDC 956.05/4—dc23

Manufactured in the United States of America

CPSIA Compliance Information: Batch #CWRYA23. For further information contact Rosen Publishing at 1-800-237-9932.

CONTENTS

Introduction

The terrorist attacks of September 11, 2001, on New York and Washington, D.C., sparked a worldwide reaction against terrorism, led by the United States.

The attacks of 9/11 were carried out by al-Qaeda, a global organization motivated by a desire to establish Islamic regimes around the world. For fundamentalist Islamists, the West is an enemy both because of its colonial past and because they believe that values such as democracy and civil rights are contrary to the Koran, the holy book of Islam. The vast majority of the world's 1.5 billion Muslims disagree with such an interpretation of the Koran and completely reject violence.

The Course of the War

In 2002, U.S. president George W. Bush launched what he called a "war on terror." Its initial target was al-Qaeda, whose leaders were in hiding in Afghanistan. A U.S.-led coalition invaded and toppled the Islamist Taliban government. The conflict also spread to other countries. In particular, U.S. leaders identified the Iraqi regime of Saddam Hussein as a potential source of terrorism. In 2003, they invaded Iraq and overthrew Saddam. However, coalition troops faced an insurgency by Islamist fighters. In Afghanistan, too, the Taliban continued to fight. A form of democratic government was established in both countries, but a decade after the start of the "war," it was not clear whether it was being won—or whether it could be won. Terrorists continued to mount attacks in Europe and elsewhere.

About This Book

This book contains two types of timelines. Along the bottom of the pages is a timeline that covers the whole period. It lists key dates and developments, color coded to indicate their part in the war. Each chapter also has its own timeline, which runs vertically down the sides of the pages. This timeline gives more specific information about the particular subject of the chapter. IN FOCUS spreads detail key organizations and events.

U.S. soldiers detonate explosives in the desert in the Horn of Africa in 2004 during Operation Enduring Freedom.

September 11

Most Americans were unaware of the Islamist group known as al-Qaeda until a series of spectacular terrorist attacks on September 11, 2001.

➔ Smoke billows from the North Tower of the World Trade Center as the second airliner strikes the South Tower.

TIMELINE **2000 JANUARY–DECEMBER**

KEY: Iraq | Afghanistan | International

January 3 Jordan
Planned attacks on three targets are thwarted; al-Qaeda is blamed for the plot.

January — May

January 3 United States
Al-Qaeda is suspected of being behind a failed plot to bomb Los Angeles International Airport.

At 8:46 a.m. on the morning of September 11, 2001, a hijacked airliner crashed into the North Tower of the World Trade Center in New York. Seventeen minutes later, another aircraft flew into the South Tower. The Twin Towers later collapsed, as did another building in the complex. At 9:37 a.m., a third aircraft crashed into the Pentagon in Washington, D.C. A fourth passenger airliner crashed in a field in Pennsylvania at 10:03 a.m.; it was later learned that passengers had fought with the hijackers, whose target was probably the White House or the Capitol building in Washington, D.C.

In all, some 2,996 people died, including the 19 hijackers, all the people on the four aircraft, and more than 340 New York City firefighters who were trying to rescue people from the World Trade Center when the buildings collapsed. Citizens from more than 90 countries died in the attacks.

Chief Suspects

Within just a few hours, the FBI, Federal Bureau of Investigation, had identified the hijackers

KEY DATES

8:46 a.m. September 11, 2001 American Airlines Flight 11 from Boston's Logan Airport, bound for Los Angeles, hits the North Tower of the World Trade Center in New York City.

9:03 a.m. United Airlines Flight 175 bound for Los Angeles hits the South Tower of the World Trade Center, New York City.

9:05 a.m. At Booker Elementary School, Sarasota, Florida, President Bush is told "America is under attack."

9:37 a.m. American Airlines Flight 77 from Washington to Los Angeles crashes into the west side of the Pentagon.

Continued on page 9

Two of the terrorists pass through airport security on the morning of the attacks.

September

December

September 28 Israel
The Palestinians begin a new intifada, or uprising, against Israeli occupation.

October 20 Yemen
In an al-Qaeda attack, the U.S. Navy destroyer USS *Cole* is rammed by a small boat carrying explosives, killing 17 sailors and injuring 39.

December 5 Jordan
A Jordanian is sentenced to death for planning millennium attacks on U.S. and Israeli targets.

Flight 93

The only one of the four hijacked airplanes to miss its intended target was Flight 93. The passengers onboard learned about the other hijackings from calls to loved ones made on the airphones. The passengers decided to act to overpower the hijackers and take control of the flight deck. Their efforts crashed the plane into a field in Pennsylvania. All 44 passengers, including the four hijackers, were killed.

responsible for the attacks. Their ringleader was Mohamed Atta, from Egypt; the others were also Arabs, including 15 from Saudi Arabia. They had spent some months in the United States before boarding the flights at Boston, Newark, and Washington, D.C. Evidence linked the hijackers to an Islamist group known as al-Qaeda, led by the Saudi Osama bin Laden. Bin Laden financed the suicide plot, which was planned by another al-Qaeda leader, Khalid Sheikh Mohammed.

An Enemy of America

Al-Qaeda had been founded by Osama bin Laden in 1979 in Afghanistan, where Muslim fighters were resisting the Soviet invasion. After the Soviets left Afghanistan in 1989, bin Laden turned his attention to the United States. In 1996, he announced that all U.S. forces should leave Saudi

→ Firefighters in New York in the aftermath of the 9/11 attacks.

TIMELINE **2000 JANUARY–JUNE**

KEY: Iraq · Afghanistan · International

January

February 1 Great Britain
A new antiterrorism act bans 21 militant groups suspected of supporting terrorism.

February 16 Iraq
U.S. and British aircraft launch bombing raids on Iraqi air defenses.

March

April 6 United States
An Algerian, Ahmed Ressam, is convicted of trying to blow up Los Angeles International Airport in 2000.

An Indonesian artist displays his portrait of Osama bin Laden.

Continued from page 7

9:57 a.m. Passengers revolt on hijacked United Airlines Flight 93 from Newark.

9:58 a.m. South Tower of the World Trade Center starts to collapse.

10:03 a.m. Flight 93 crashes into a field in Pennsylvania.

10:10 a.m. Part of the west side of the Pentagon collapses.

10:28 a.m. The North Tower of the World Trade Center collapses 1 hour, 41 minutes, and 45 seconds after the plane's impact.

10:43 a.m. Mayor Rudolph Giuliani orders the evacuation of Lower Manhattan.

8:30 p.m. President Bush addresses the nation from the White House.

11:30 p.m. President Bush notes in his journal that the Americans suspect Osama bin Laden of the attacks.

Arabia, where they had been based since the Persian Gulf War against Iraq in 1990. In 1998, he issued further threats against the United States. That same year, al-Qaeda bombed the U.S. Embassies in Kenya and Tanzania.

Bin Laden was believed to be sheltered by the radical Islamic Taliban government in Afghanistan. The United States gathered a broad alliance to help topple the Taliban and capture bin Laden. At the same time, the PATRIOT Act gave the U.S. government greater powers to monitor suspected terrorists at home, despite complaints that the provisions interfered with civil liberties.

A monument marks the site where Flight 93 crashed.

May 26 Afghanistan
The U.N. Security Council reports that the Taliban is selling heroin and opium to raise funds to train terrorists.

May

June

May 9 Afghanistan
The Taliban close U.N. offices in retaliation for the imposition of United Nations sanctions.

June 15 India
Security forces disrupt bombers sent by al-Qaeda to attack the U.S. Embassy in New Delhi.

IN FOCUS

Islamic Terrorist Movements

There were many radical Islamist terrorist groups that formed in the world in the early 21st century.

1

The attack on the World Trade Center and other U.S. targets on September 11, 2001, was carried out by al-Qaeda. Its members were Islamic radicals who did not feel themselves bound by any national allegiances. Most of them felt that they were fighting for the return of what they called the caliphate, a political union of all Muslim believers. Many young men had become radicalized during the 1990s, when Muslims in Bosnia were attacked. Others were concerned about a long-running grievance in the form of the state of Israel, which they felt was a violation of a previously Islamic territory.

2

Poverty and Opportunity

Poverty in the Islamic world and lack of opportunities for young Muslim males provided a fertile ground for recruitment into radical organizations. There were institutions in many states (such as the security services in Pakistan) that encouraged them. The state of Iran funded terrorist groups, particularly Hezbollah in the Gaza Strip and Lebanon. This background provided terrorist organizations, institutions, and the states that encouraged them with a pool of recruits. The United States and its allies were trying to fight and control a many-headed and flexible opponent with many members that could pop up anywhere without warning.

KEY DATES

1985 Hezbollah is founded in Lebanon with support from Iran. The name was chosen by Iranian leader Ayatollah Khomeini.

1988 Osama bin Laden founds al-Qaeda.

1996 Taliban take over in Afghanistan and enforce a strict interpretation of Islam on the entire country. They are pushed from power after the allied invasion of 2001.

May 2009 Al-Shabab carries out its first attacks in Somalia, proclaiming affiliation to al-Qaeda.

June 2014 Islamic State proclaims itself to be a worldwide caliphate.

August 2021 Taliban again take control of Afghanistan.

1 A Madrasah, an Islamic school, in Indonesia. The influence of teachers in such Madrasahs has been much debated.

2 The ruins of the city of Mosul after ISIS was forced out of the city by the 2017 "Nineveh" offensive.

3 A car burns in Strasbourg, France, set on fire during a night of rioting by disaffected young Muslim men.

4 A Muslim grave digger in Bosnia, where genocidal attacks on the Islamic community radicalized many young Muslims.

The War on Terror Begins

The first target of the U.S. campaign was Osama bin Laden's al-Qaeda, which was sheltered by the Taliban government of Afghanistan.

↑ Northern Alliance fighters ride into Kabul after the Taliban fled the Afghan capital.

TIMELINE 2001 JULY-DECEMBER

KEY: Iraq | Afghanistan | International

September 11 United States Al-Qaeda terrorists fly hijacked airliners into the World Trade Center in New York City and the Pentagon in Washington, D.C. A fourth plane crashes in a field in Pennsylvania; some 2,996 people are killed.

October 16 Mediterranean
Operation Active Endeavor begins; it is NATO's naval operation to prevent terrorist activities in the Mediterranean.

July

October

October 7 Afghanistan
Troops of the U.S.-led coalition invade Afghanistan.

November 9 Afghanistan
In the Battle of Mazar-i- Sharif, the U.S. beats the Taliban to take the most important city in northern Afghanistan.

On September 20, 2001, George W. Bush told the U.S. Congress that "our war on terror begins with al-Qaeda, but it does not end there. It will not end until every terrorist group of global reach has been found, stopped, and defeated." Later, in January 2002, Bush went on to identify an "axis of evil": countries that used or would potentially be prepared to use terrorism as part of state strategy—Iran, Iraq, and North Korea.

The Taliban

In the immediate aftermath of the attacks of 9/11, the United States' first target was Osama bin Laden and the Taliban government that harbored him in Afghanistan. The Taliban had come to power in 1996, following the withdrawal of Soviet troops from Afghanistan.

KEY DATES

September 20, 2001 President George W. Bush uses the phrase "war on terror" in an address to Congress.

September 22, 2001 Saudi Arabia and the United Arab Emirates withdraw recognition of the Taliban as the government of Afghanistan; now only Pakistan acknowledges the government.

October 7, 2001 U.S. and British jets begin bombing targets in Afghanistan.

November 9, 2001 Northern Alliance forces claim the city of Mazar-i- Sharif.

November 13, 2001 Northern Alliance forces enter the Afghan capital, Kabul, after it is abandoned by the Taliban.

November 25, 2001 U.S. forces establish their first base in Afghanistan, Camp Rhino.

Continued on page 15

Cleanup continues at "Ground Zero," the site of the World Trade Center.

November 12–25 Afghanistan Kunduz falls to alliance troops. It is the last Taliban garrison in the north of Afghanistan.

December

December 7 Afghanistan Coalition forces conquer Kandahar, the last Taliban stronghold in the country.

December 13 India Islamist gunmen attack Parliament in New Delhi; India blames the attack on Pakistan-based groups.

December 22 United States Richard Reid, a British Islamic fundamentalist, tries but fails to detonate explosives hidden in his shoe on a transatlantic flight.

December 22 Afghanistan Hamid Karzai becomes the head of a power-sharing government.

Al-Qaeda

The chief target of Operation Enduring Freedom, al-Qaeda, was blamed for terror attacks around the world. It had been created in the late 1980s by the Saudi Osama bin Laden to support Muslims fighting the Soviet occupation of Afghanistan. Bin Laden's vast wealth allowed him to fund the organization with up to $30 million a year. Al-Qaeda, which means "the base" in Arabic, now encourages terrorist attacks aimed at creating strict Muslim states around the world.

These Taliban ("students") promoted a strict form of Islam. They banned music and hobbies such as kite flying, prevented women from working or men from shaving, and blew up huge Buddhist statues that were recognized as a World Heritage Site by the United Nations. The Taliban had offered Osama bin Laden a safe haven after other Muslim countries had expelled him for his increasingly radical speeches and threats. Bin Laden's aim of creating fundamentalist Islamic states threatened moderate Muslim governments as much as it did Western governments.

Into Afghanistan

After the 9/11 attacks, the North Atlantic Treaty Organization (NATO) announced that it recognized the attack on the United States as an attack on all its members. There was a similar response from other parts of the world. The United States put together a coalition that was supported by dozens of nations, either in terms of military forces, supplies, bases, or in permission for use of air bases. On Sunday, October 7, 2001, U.S.

➔ George W. Bush declared a "war on terror" in January 2002.

TIMELINE 2002 JANUARY-JUNE

KEY: Iraq | Afghanistan | International

January — March

January 1 Afghanistan
The first foreign peacekeepers arrive in Afghanistan.

January 15 Philippines
Operation Enduring Freedom begins in the Philippines.

January 29 United States
In his State of the Union address, George Bush identifies an "axis of evil" of Iran, Iraq, and North Korea.

February 1 Pakistan
Islamic militants behead kidnapped U.S. journalist Daniel Pearl.

A young Afghan watches as U.S. soldiers search for al-Qaeda suspects in his home.

and British aircraft started bombing Taliban targets. The coalition campaign was aided by the Northern Alliance, a group of Afghan warlords in the north of the country that resented Taliban rule. The initial phase of the ground war was completed by November 26. Many of the Taliban fled to Pakistan. However, in the Battle of Tora Bora, U.S. forces apparently missed an opportunity to capture Osama bin Laden.

A Wider Operation

As Operation Enduring Freedom began in Afghanistan, other parts of the operation began in countries that also feared Islamic extremism. They included operations in the Philippines, the Horn of Africa, the Sahara region, and later in the Caribbean and Kyrgyzstan.

Continued from page 13

January 29, 2002 President George W. Bush identifies an "axis of evil"—Iran, Iraq, and North Korea—as potential sponsors of terrorism and targets for U.S. operations.

January 16, 2002 The United Nations Security Council starts an arms embargo on Afghanistan and freezes assets belonging to Osama bin Laden.

January 15, 2002 Some 1,200 U.S. special forces arrive in the Philippines as part of Operation Enduring Freedom.

March 11, 2002 George W. Bush offers U.S. assistance to any government to combat terrorism.

June 7, 2002 George W. Bush reveals plans for increased homeland security.

October 7, 2002 NATO forces arrive to advance Operation Enduring Freedom in the Horn of Africa.

April 11 Tunisia
An al-Qaeda suicide bomber drives a gas tanker into a synagogue, killing 21 people.

May

May 9 Russia
A bomb explosion at Victory Day celebrations in Dagestan kills 42 people.

June

June 13 Afghanistan
The Loya Jirga tribal assembly chooses Hamid Karzai as the president.

June 14 Pakistan
A car bomb near the U.S. Embassy in Karachi kills 12 people.

Afghanistan

When the Americans led the coalition invasion of Afghanistan in 2001, little did U.S. leaders know that the war would be continuing 10 years later.

French soldiers of NATO's International Security Assistance Force patrol in Afghanistan.

TIMELINE 2002 JULY–DECEMBER

KEY: Iraq | Afghanistan | International

July — October

September 12 United States
President George W. Bush warns the United Nations of the growing threat from Iraq.

October 12 Indonesia
Bombs in the tourist resort of Bali kill 202 people, many of whom are Westerners and Australians.

October 23–26 Russia
Chechen separatists seize hostages in a theater in Moscow; a rescue operation leaves 120 hostages and 40 terrorists dead.

After al-Qaeda's September 11, 2001, attacks, the United States launched a war in Afghanistan to destroy the terrorist bases there and overthrow the Taliban, the country's fundamentalist Muslim rulers who harbored bin Laden. The campaign went well as the Taliban were removed from power and a pro-Western government was installed in the capital, Kabul.

To escape the U.S.-led war in Afghanistan, al-Qaeda's leadership sought refuge across the border in Pakistan's tribal areas. Bin Laden, along with other members of the organization, went into hiding in Pakistan, where he was located and killed by U.S. special forces in 2011.

NATO in Afghanistan

As part of the war on terror, the United States was helped in Afghanistan by other members of the North Atlantic Treaty Organization (NATO). Since September 11, 2001, the allies have sought to create a "new" NATO, able to go beyond Europe to combat new threats, such as terrorism and the proliferation of weapons of mass destruction.

Triumphant Northern Alliance troops enter Kabul on November 13, 2001.

KEY DATES

February 15, 1989 The Soviets withdraw from Afghanistan.

September 27, 1996 The Taliban seize Kabul.

September 11, 2001 Al-Qaeda terrorist attacks occur in the United States.

October 7, 2001 Operation Enduring Freedom is launched by the United States to destroy al-Qaeda safe havens, including those in Afghanistan.

November 13, 2001 Kabul falls to Northern Alliance.

December 3–17, 2001 Al-Qaeda members are forced out of the Tora Bora cave complex and escape to Pakistan.

December 22, 2001 Hamid Karzai is sworn in as head of an interim government.

Continued on page 19

November

November 18 Iraq United Nations weapons inspectors arrive in Iraq to search for evidence of weapons of mass destruction.

November 28 Kenya A bomb attack on a hotel leaves 15 people dead.

December

December 27 Russia A bus bomb is used to blow up the Chechen parliament in Grozny, killing 83 people.

Battle of Tora Bora

Tora Bora is an ancient and vast cave complex near the Khyber Pass. Believing Osama bin Laden and his followers were hiding in the caves, Afghan forces attacked Tora Bora with the U.S. Air Force providing air support in early December 2001. On December 12, Afghan commanders opened negotiations with members of al-Qaeda. These talks led to many of them, including Osama bin Laden, being allowed to escape west into Pakistan.

Afghanistan is NATO's first "out of area" mission beyond Europe. The purpose of the mission is the stabilization and reconstruction of Afghanistan.

The NATO-led International Security Assistance Force (ISAF) faced many obstacles: shoring up a weak government in Kabul; using military capabilities in a distant country with rugged terrain; and also rebuilding a country devastated by war and troubled by a resilient narcotics trade. Although the allies agree on ISAF's mission goals, they differ on how to accomplish them. At first, only the United States wanted to engage directly in the destruction of poppy fields and drug facilities in attempts to destroy the illegal drug trade.

Rebuilding Afghanistan

The PRTs, or Provincial Reconstruction Teams, made up of military and civilian officials, are charged with extending the reach of the

A U.S. patrol explores the remote mountains of Kandahar province in 2009.

TIMELINE 2003 JANUARY–JUNE

KEY: Iraq | Afghanistan | International

January

January 5 Israel
Two Islamist bombers kill 23 people in coordinated attacks in Tel Aviv.

March

March 4 Philippines
A bomb blast at Davao leaves 21 dead.

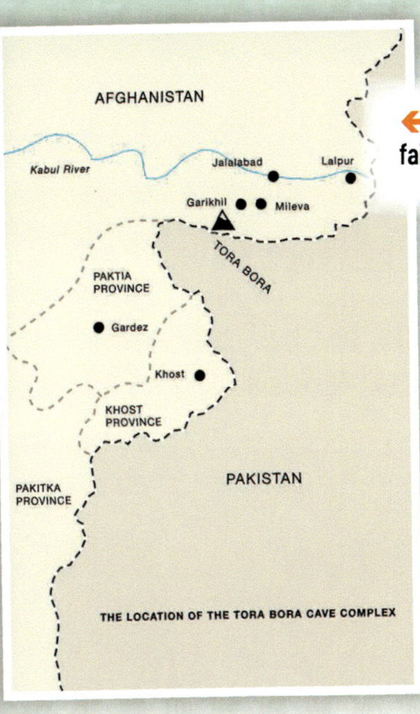

The U.S. attack on Tora Bora failed to trap the al-Qaeda leaders.

Afghan government by improving governance and rebuilding the economy. There are differences in how individual NATO governments operate their PRTs. Turmoil in Pakistan complicates efforts to prevent the Taliban infiltrating Afghanistan.

Talking to the Taliban?

By 2008, it appeared that NATO's military effort in Afghanistan was failing. Violence in and around Kabul reached record highs, corruption was rampant, and pessimism rose. A U.S. report said Afghanistan was in a "downward spiral," fueled by drug money and weak central government. It appeared that the only solution to the war in Afghanistan was a settlement with the Taliban, but talking to their enemy was something the Americans did not relish.

Continued from page 17

August 11, 2003 NATO takes over responsibility for security in Kabul, its first such duty outside Europe.

September 2005 Parliamentary elections held in Afghanistan for the first time in 30 years.

May–June 2006 Many Taliban killed in Operation Mountain Thrust in the south.

March 2007 Operation Achilles is another large thrust against the Taliban in the south.

September 2008 President Bush sends an extra 4,500 U.S. troops to Afghanistan.

July 2009 U.S. and Afghan forces begin a major operation in Helmand province.

July 2010 President Karzai formulates plan for Afghan forces to take charge of security by 2014.

March 17 Iraq President George Bush gives Saddam Hussein 48 hours to leave Iraq or face war.

March 20 Iraq A U.S.-led military invasion topples the government of Saddam Hussein, who goes into hiding.

May

May 12 Saudi Arabia Al-Qaeda is blamed for suicide bomb attacks on compounds for U.S. workers in Riyadh that kill 26 people.

IN FOCUS

Withdrawal from Afghanistan

The Afghanistan War was long and difficult. In the end, the United States decided to pull out its final troops.

1

By the time Barack Obama came to the U.S. presidency in 2009, the war in Afghanistan seemed unwinnable. Obama temporarily increased troop numbers and although there were still some successes, such as the pinpointing of Osama bin Laden's hideout in Pakistan and the attack there that killed him in 2011, the war dragged on. In 2014, responsibility for the fighting was formally transferred to the Afghan army. In spite of popular policies such as the recovery of women's rights and widespread extension of education, the central government lacked legitimacy and was extremely corrupt. Afghans owed allegiance to tribal and ethnic groups, considering themselves Pushtun, Tajik, or Uzbek rather than citizens of the central government.

2

Return of the Taliban

The Taliban increased their hold in the countryside. When President Trump took office in 2017, he wanted to end U.S. involvement and signed an agreement about U.S. withdrawal with the Taliban in February 2020. Finally, in 2021, under President Joe Biden, U.S. troops withdrew completely. Intelligence estimates had concluded that the Afghan army could resist the Taliban, but the army soon collapsed and President Ashraf Ghani fled the country. Amid chaotic scenes at Kabul airport, U.S. nationals and many Afghans were evacuated while the Taliban marched into Kabul itself, coming back to power after over 20 years of constant fighting in the war-torn country.

3

4

KEY DATES

May 1, 2011 Osama bin Laden is killed by U.S. Special Forces in Pakistan.

September 2014 Mohammed Ashraf Ghani becomes president of Afghanistan.

December 28, 2014 NATO formally ends combat operations in Afghanistan.

February 27, 2018 President Ashraf Ghani calls for unconditional peace talks with the Taliban.

February 2020 U.S. and the Taliban sign a deal requiring U.S. troops to withdraw by April 2021.

August 30, 2021 Final U.S. evacuation flight leaves Kabul airport.

1 President Ashraf Ghani of Afghanistan (left) meets President Trump during Ghani's visit to the United States.

2 U.S. troops cover Afghans who are making their way to Kabul airport in an attempt to escape to safety.

3 Secretary of State Mike Pompeo (center) meets the Taliban delegation during talks with the U.S. government in 2019-2020.

4 American envoy Zalmay Khalilzad (second from left) signs the 2020 agreement with the Taliban by which the United States agrees to withdraw its troops from Afghanistan.

Africa

The continuing rise of homegrown terrorism across Africa is a cause of grave concern to the United States as the reach of al-Qaeda appears to grow stronger.

➔ A U.S. soldier befriends a group of curious children in Djibouti, in the Horn of Africa, in March 2004.

TIMELINE 2003 JULY–DECEMBER

KEY: Iraq | Afghanistan | International

July

July 13 Iraq
A U.S.-appointed governing council meets for the first time.

August

August 11 Afghanistan
NATO takes control of security in the capital, Kabul.

August 19 Iraq
A suicide bombing wrecks the United Nations headquarters in Baghdad, killing the senior U.N. representative in the country.

August 25 India
Two separate bombs in Mumbai kill a total of 50 people.

At the start of the 21st century, the U.S. military embarked on a long-term push into Africa to stop what it considered to be growing inroads by al-Qaeda and other terrorist networks in poor, lawless, and largely Muslim expanses of Algeria, Chad, Mali, Mauritania, Niger, Senegal, Nigeria, Morocco, and Tunisia.

Terrorism in the Horn of Africa

The thrust into Africa was considered to be vital in order to head off infiltration by international terrorist groups. Small groups of Islamic radicals were moving into Africa from the conflict in Iraq, where Africans made up about a quarter of the foreign fighters.

Soldiers wait to defend the Somali capital against Islamists in 2010.

KEY DATES

October 12, 2000 The USS *Cole* is attacked by a suicide bomber in the Yemeni port of Aden; 17 U.S. sailors are killed.

November 28, 2002 In the coastal town of Mombasa, Kenya, the Army of Palestine, a previously unknown Lebanese group, bombs Israeli-owned targets; the United States condemns the attacks and vows to continue its "war on terror."

July 23, 2005 Following suicide bombings by a group claiming ties to al-Qaeda, which kill at least 88 people at the Egyptian resort of Sharm el-Sheik, the United States denounces continuing terror attacks.

Continued on page 25

November

December

November 8 Saudi Arabia An expatriate living compound in al-Muhaya is attacked by a car bomb that kills 17 people.

December 5 Russia Suicide bombers attack a train in southern Russia, killing 46 people.

December 14 Iraq Saddam Hussein is captured. He was hiding in a hole in the ground near Tikrit.

Sudan

Sudan became the site of an ideological struggle between the United States and al-Qaeda. Sudan supported the "war on terror" but suffered from the expansion of al-Qaeda's presence in the country. By 2008, it was ranked as the third most unstable country in the world. In a referendum in January 2011, people in southern Sudan—who are not Muslim—voted to split from the North.

Somalia

Somalia has given the most cause for concern. U.S. strategy toward Somalia was threefold: to eliminate the terrorist threat, to promote political stability, and to address the humanitarian crisis. Somalia proved far more complex than either the United States or its Ethiopian allies admitted, however. Since 1991, there has been no stable government. The Islamic Courts Union, which was the effective Somali government, was not recognized internationally but had popular support within Somalia, where it controlled most of the country.

Ongoing Violence

Ethiopia had secretly stationed troops in Somalia and, with U.S. backing, invaded its neighbor in 2007. Ethiopian troops quit Somalia in January 2009, shortly before a moderate Islamist Somali

A U.S. C-130 Hercules transport aircraft takes off from a Sudanese airfield.

TIMELINE 2004 JANUARY–JUNE

KEY: Iraq | Afghanistan | International

January

February 6 Russia
A blast on the Moscow metro during rush hour kills 41 people.

February 27 Iraq
Insurgent attacks claim 27 victims in Fallujah.

March

March 2 Iraq
Some 170 people die in attacks on Shia holy sites in Baghdad and Karbala.

March 11 Spain
Bombs detonated on commuter trains in Madrid kill 191 people.

→ Portuguese marines detain suspects in the Gulf of Aden.

government was elected. The government was weak, however, and soon collapsed. In May 2009, Islamists again attacked the capital. The radical group al-Shabab proclaimed its allegiance to al-Qaeda and carried out a series of terrorist attacks.

U.N. Secretary-General Ban Ki-moon called for international support to bring stability to Somalia. However, Somali unrest spread to other parts of East Africa. In July 2010, al-Shabab bombed Kampala, the Ugandan capital, killing 74 people watching the World Cup final on TV. Religious and ethnic divisions continued to divide Sudan. Meanwhile, al-Qaeda still operated in the region, supported by al-Shabab.

→ A Kenyan Muslim protests the deportation of a preacher suspected of terrorism.

↓ Continued from page 23

April 23, 2006 Osama bin Laden criticizes a peace agreement in Sudan that had been made between the military-Islamist government and the Sudan People's Liberation Movement (SPLM) in January 2005.

June 11, 2007 President George W. Bush gives $1 billion in military and other aid to Kenya; a car bomb explodes near the U.S. Embassy in Nairobi, the capital.

July 10, 2010 A bomb kills 74 people watching the World Cup finals in a bar in the Ugandan capital, Kampala; an Islamist Somali group with ties to al-Qaeda claims to have carried out the attack.

January 1, 2011 Islamic extremists bomb a Coptic church in Alexandria, Egypt, killing 23 Christian worshipers.

April 3 Spain
The Madrid railroad bombers blow themselves up when they are cornered by police in Madrid.

April–May Iraq
The Mehdi Army, Shia militia loyal to Mullah Moqtada al-Sadr, take on coalition forces in Iraq.

May

May 9 Russia
The president of Chechnya is killed by a bomb at a stadium where he is attending a public event.

June 28 Iraq
U.S. forces hand sovereignty in Iraq to the interim Iraqi government.

IN FOCUS Al-Shabab and Africa

North and east Africa has suffered many terrorist attacks on civilian infrastructure and even on schools.

1

Al-Shabab originally came to prominence in Somalia, and even though it has never threatened to take power, it has been able to mount some deadly terrorist attacks, such as bombing shopping malls in 2013 in Kenya and then in Mogadishu in 2017. There were probably over 5,000 al-Shabab members active in East Africa in the early 2020s. They have links with al-Qaeda, particularly an offshoot known as al-Qaeda in Islamic Mahgreb, although relations between these groups have been strained at times.

Boko Haram

Al-Shabab also has links with terrorist groups farther west across Africa, notably the group Boko Haram. This is a terrorist group based in northeast Nigeria, which began an insurgency in 2009. It had links with Islamic State (ISIS) and has destabilized large areas of Nigeria. Its single most notorious act was the abduction of 276 Nigerian schoolgirls in 2014. But Boko Haram has attacked many other schools, and carried out low-level attacks on government institutions.

Effectively, much of Africa south of the Sahara has been ravaged by terrorist groups since 2010, with the governments there finding it difficult to root out the highly motivated Islamic fighters. Since 2020, for a time, France helped some governments with special forces units. More recently, Russia has allowed an organization known as the Wagner Group (largely consisting of former Russian soldiers) to find employment with governments there to take on Islamist terrorist groups.

2

3

4

KEY DATES

May 2009 Al-Shabab carries out its first attacks in Somalia, proclaiming affiliation to al-Qaeda and enjoying early success.

August 2011 Al-Shabab is driven out of Mogadishu, the Somali capital.

September 1, 2014 Al-Shabab leader Ahmed Abdi Godane killed in U.S. drone strike.

December 28, 2019 Al-Shabab carries out a suicide truck bombing in Mogadishu. The dead total 85; 140 people are injured.

2021 Boko Haram attacks Nigerian Army positions in Borno State, northeast Nigeria.

January-April 2022 Wagner Group soldiers from Russia take part in operations with forces of the Mali government against Islamist rebels. They take the town of Moura and over 300 local men are dead after the Islamists fled.

1 Under an amnesty in Somalia, some al-Shabab fighters agreed to lay down their arms in 2012.

2 The state of Nigeria reeled from the kidnapping of hundreds of schoolgirls at Chibok by Boko Haram in 2014.

3 Parents of the girls abducted in the 2014 mass kidnapping express their fears for the lives of their children.

4 Smoke billows from the Westgate Shopping Mall in Nairobi, where four al-Shabab militants made an attack. Over 60 civilians were killed in this episode.

Europe

In the first decade of this century, bombs across Europe brought the realities of the Islamist war home to Europeans. Many of the terrorists were homegrown.

➔ A suicide bomb tore the roof off this London bus in the terrorist attacks of July 7, 2005.

TIMELINE **2004 JULY–DECEMBER**

KEY: Iraq | Afghanistan | International

July

August 5–27 Iraq
Intense fighting continues in Najaf between U.S. forces and Shia militia of Moqtada al-Sadr.

September

September 1 Russia
Separatist terrorists seize a school at Beslan, in North Ossetia, taking 1,100 people hostage; in a rescue operation three days later, 334 hostages die.

September 16 Afghanistan
Taliban fire a rocket at a helicopter carrying President Hamid Karzai.

A U.S. soldier hands out counterterrorism leaflets in Bosnia

In Europe, the terrorist threat came from numerous sources. In Spain, Basque nationalists continued an armed campaign against the government. In Northern Ireland, the Continuity IRA attacked Protestant targets. However, in both cases the peak of violence had passed.

Elsewhere, nationalism combined with Islamism in struggles in the Caucasus region of southern Russia, where separatists from republics such as Chechnya fought against Russian control. In 2002, Chechen terrorists seized a theater audience as hostages in the Russian capital, Moscow. In the police operation that followed, hundreds of hostages died. There were

A shrine to the children who died in the Beslan school siege.

KEY DATES

October 23, 2002 Armed Chechen attackers seize a crowded Moscow theater; in a later rescue attempt, at least 120 hostages die.

February 6, 2004 Suicide bombers on the Moscow metro kill at least 40 people.

March 11, 2004 Al-Qaeda supporters blow up commuter trains in Madrid, Spain, killing 191 people.

September 1, 2004 Armed Chechen separatists attack a school in Beslan, South Russia; in an attempted rescue, 334 hostages die, including 186 of the children.

Continued on page 31

October 7 Pakistan A car bomb kills 38 people at a Sunni religious rally.

December 19 Iraq A car bomb attack on a funeral procession in Najaf kills around 50 people.

October

December

November 7 Iraq U.S. and Iraqi troops launch Operation Phantom Fury, a major campaign against insurgents in Fallujah.

also numerous suicide bombings on the Moscow metro. The most notorious Chechen attack came in 2004, when terrorists took hundreds of children and parents hostage in a school in Beslan, North Ossetia. Again, the police operation went wrong: some 334 hostages died. More than half of them were young children.

Western Europe

In western Europe, the Islamist threat was both internal and external. Muslim terrorists from North Africa were active in southern Europe, but many European countries produced homegrown terrorists. Young Muslims turned against the countries where they were raised. Often such

Jean Charles de Menezes

On July 22, 2005, de Menezes, a Brazilian man living in London, was identified by antiterrorist police as a fugitive involved in failed bomb attacks in the city the previous day. The police followed him to a subway station, where they shot him dead. He was later found to be an innocent victim of mistaken identity. The British police were fined for the killing. The shoot-to-kill policy that had been adopted to deal with suicide bombers was abandoned.

➔ Badly destroyed rail carriages following the Madrid bombings.

TIMELINE 2005 JANUARY–JUNE

KEY: Iraq | Afghanistan | International

January — March

January 30 Iraq
Millions of Iraqis vote in elections for a national assembly.

February 14 Lebanon
A car bomb kills the former prime minister of Lebanon and some 20 other people.

February 28 Iraq
In Hilla, Baghdad, a car bomb leaves 114 people dead.

Supporters of Jean Charles de Menezes call for an inquiry into his shooting by U.K. police.

individuals were motivated by resentment of Western support for Israel and interference in the Muslim world. North Africans blew up commuter trains in Madrid, Spain, in 2004 in retaliation for Spain's support for the invasion of Iraq. In 2005, British Muslims attacked subway trains and buses in London.

Successful Intelligence

Within Europe, the war on terror was largely an intelligence operation. Security forces disrupted a number of more or less serious plots before they were realized. There were also some attacks that failed due to the lack of skill of the terrorists.

Continued from page 29

July 7, 2005 Suicide bombers target London with bombs on three subway trains and one bus; 52 people die.

August 10, 2006 A plot to blow up U.S.-bound aircraft midflight is foiled in London.

June 27, 2007 A car rams into a terminal at Scotland's Glasgow Airport in a failed suicide bombing.

March 29, 2010 Female suicide bombers attack the Moscow metro, killing 40.

December 11, 2010 Two bombs in Stockholm, Sweden, kill the bomber.

January 24, 2011 A suicide bomber attacks Moscow's Domodedovo Airport, killing at least 35 people.

May

May Iraq
Some 672 civilians die in bomb attacks during May, representing a huge surge in the number of attacks.

April Egypt
A number of attacks in April target tourist buses and markets frequented by tourists.

IN FOCUS

Bombs and Knife Attacks

European cities were subject to various attacks by terrorists who used bombs, vehicles, and sometimes knives.

After the initial years of the War on Terror, European states found themselves with the difficult task of identifying individuals who were likely to commit terrorist acts within their societies. Large numbers of young Muslim men were potential recruits into terrorist organizations. Even when individuals were identified, programs to rehabilitate likely offenders were no guarantee of success: in 2019 Usman Khan, a man who had been cleared as having completed rehabilitation, attacked and killed two people in London, U.K.

A Series of Attacks

There were several deadly bombings. In Manchester, England, Salman Ramadan Abedi detonated a bomb he was carrying at a concert by the singer Ariana Grande in 2017. Over 1,000 people were badly injured and 23 died.

Attacks with knives occurred on several occasions in the U.K., France, and Germany. France has a large Muslim population concentrated in poor living conditions. For the period 2015 to 2018 alone, 249 people were killed in 22 terrorist attacks. The deadliest was in November 2015 when three groups coordinated attacks in Paris, and 130 people died. In Germany, there were nine attacks in the years from 2015 to 2020.

KEY DATES

November 13, 2015 Terror attacks in Paris. One group attacks a soccer stadium, a second fires randomly into cafés and restaurants in the city, while a third attacks the Bataclan Theater. Deaths total 130, with over 400 people injured.

March 22, 2016 Terrorists affiliated to ISIS make two attacks on Brussels airport and one on a metro station. They kill 32 people and more than 300 are injured.

December 19, 2016 Terrorists drive a truck into a Christmas market in Berlin. They kill 12 people and dozens are injured.

June 3, 2017 Three terrorists drive a van at pedestrians on London Bridge and crash it near the busy Borough Market. They run into the market, stabbing eight people to death and wounding 48 more before being shot dead by police.

July 28, 2017 A failed Palestinian asylum seeker attacks people with a knife in a supermarket in Hamburg, Germany. He kills one man and injures six others.

1 The Breitscheidplatz in Berlin is cordoned off after the incident in 2016 when a truck was driven into a crowded Christmas market.

2 St Ann's Square in Manchester, England, decorated with flowers for the dead of the 2017 Manchester bombing.

3 The two men in the left of the photograph are believed to have carried out the bombing of Brussels airport in 2015.

4 Mourners gather in Paris to remember the people who died in the terrorist attacks of November 2015.

India and Pakistan

Religious tensions that have marked the relationship between India and Pakistan since Partition in 1947 have worsened in the last decade.

Mumbai's famous Taj Mahal Palace hotel on fire during the terrorist attacks of 2008.

TIMELINE 2005 JULY–DECEMBER

KEY: Iraq | Afghanistan | International

July

July 7 Britain
A coordinated suicide bomb attack on London's transportation system kills 52 people.

July 21 Britain
A second attempted attack on London buses and subways fails when explosives do not detonate; the suspects are arrested.

July 23 Egypt
Car bombs in the Egyptian resort of Sharm el-Sheik kill 88 people.

Pakistani police guard suspected members of the Taliban near the border with Afghanistan.

Following the 9/11 attacks and the U.S.-led invasion of Afghanistan that followed, leaders of al-Qaeda and the Afghan Taliban, along with several other terrorist groups, fled across the border into Pakistan. Al-Qaeda's leader, Osama bin Laden, eventually settled in the Pakistani city of Abottabad. At the start of May 2011 he was shot dead there when U.S. special forces raided his secret compound.

The Taliban dominated the northwestern Swat Valley, from where it was suspected of launching various terrorist attacks on targets in major Pakistani cities. The Taliban vowed to increase its attacks after the August 2009 killing by a U.S. drone (unmanned bomber) of its then leader, Baitullah Mehsud. Meanwhile, the lawless northwest tribal region, which acts as a sanctuary for militants, threatened to become

KEY DATES

August 25, 2003 In Mumbai, India, two car bombs near the Gateway of India and Zaveri bazaar kill 54 people.

October 7, 2004 In Multan, Pakistan, a car bomb kills 38 at a Sunni religious rally.

October 29, 2005 Three explosions in New Delhi, India, kill 60 and injure more than 200.

March 7, 2006 A bomb in the Hindu holy city of Varanasi, India, kills 28.

April 11, 2006 A suicide bomber kills 57 Sunni Muslims in Karachi, Pakistan.

July 11, 2006 Seven coordinated bombs explode in Mumbai, India, killing 209.

August 25, 2007 Twin bombs detonated in Hyderabad, India, kill 44 people.

Continued on page 37

October 24 Iraq
Car bombs outside the Green Zone in Baghdad kill 20 people.

September

September 18 Afghanistan
Parliamentary elections are held in Afghanistan.

The Assassination of Benazir Bhutto

Benazir Bhutto (1953-2007) was the first woman to lead an Islamic state. She served two terms as Pakistan's prime minister (1988-1990 and 1993-1996). In 2007, she returned from self-imposed exile to campaign in elections. Almost instantly, she was targeted by Islamic terrorists. She was killed at a rally in Rawalpindi on December 27, 2007. An attacker shot her before blowing himself up.

further destabilized in August 2010 by the worst floods to occur in Pakistan for 80 years, which affected some 20 million people throughout the north of the country.

The Mumbai Attacks

In November 2008, terrorists with bombs and guns attacked a range of targets in India's financial capital, Mumbai. The Indian government blamed Pakistan-based militants, further increasing tension between India and Pakistan. Yet cooperation between the two countries is vital to the "war on terror." To this end, in September 2008, the U.S. government formed a "Friends for Pakistan" group to help Pakistan with development and stability. The group includes China and Saudi Arabia, which both have a considerable influence over Pakistan's political and military elite.

➔ The Swat Valley is a base for the Taliban in Pakistan.

TIMELINE **2006 JANUARY–JUNE**

KEY: Iraq | Afghanistan | International

February 22 Iraq
A bomb attack on a Shia shrine in Samarra begins a wave of sectarian violence between Shias and Sunnis.

March 7 India
Bombs in the Hindu holy city of Varanasi leave 28 dead.

April 11 Pakistan
A suicide bomber kills 57 Sunni Muslims in Karachi.

Ajmal Kasab was the only terrorist to be caught alive after the Mumbai attacks.

The ISI Problem

The Mumbai attacks renewed suspicions that the Pakistani government, particularly its intelligence agency, the Inter-Services Intelligence (ISI), might not wholly support Washington's fight against terrorism. In May 2011 the United States gave Pakistan no warning of the special forces raid on Osama bin Laden's compound during which the terrorist was shot dead. Pakistan was forced to admit that its intelligence services had been unaware of bin Laden's presence in the country. Some voices in the U.S. administration expressed doubts that the claim could be true.

Continued from page 35

October 18, 2007 Former Pakistani prime minister, Benazir Bhutto, survives a suicide bomb attack that kills 136 followers.

December 27, 2007 Benazir Bhutto is assassinated in Rawalpindi, Pakistan.

July 7, 2008 Pakistan is blamed for a suicide attack on the Indian Embassy in Kabul that kills 50.

September 20, 2008 A car bomb at the Marriott Hotel, Islamabad, Pakistan, kills 60 and injures 250.

November 26–29, 2008 More than 10 coordinated shooting and bomb attacks across Mumbai, India, kill at least 172.

December 2008 Press reports claim that Islamic militants now control more than 75 percent of Pakistan's Swat Valley.

May 1, 2011 Osama bin Laden is killed in a U.S. special forces raid in Abbottabad, Pakistan.

An Indian commando runs for cover during the Mumbai attacks.

May

June

May–June Afghanistan
U.S. and NATO forces launch Operation Mountain Thrust against the Taliban; there are scores of dead on both sides.

June 2–3 Canada
Police in Canada arrest 17 alleged Islamic terrorists.

June 7 Iraq
The al-Qaeda leader in Iraq, Abu Musab al-Zarqawi, is killed in an American airstrike.

IN FOCUS

Iran

Since its Islamic revolution in 1979, Iran has pursued a path opposing the U.S. and Israel.

1

One of the major factors in Islamic terrorism across the Middle East has been the policies of the state of Iran. Iran underwent a revolution in 1979, when its then ruler, the pro-western Shah Reza Pahlavi, was overthrown in a popular rising. An Islamic state was established, with ultimate power resting in the hands of Islamic religious leaders, the first of whom was the Ayatollah Khomeini.

Iran was (and remains) fiercely opposed to the state of Israel and called the United States the "Great Satan" because of its involvement in the region. Iran has sponsored many terrorist groups, in particular Hezbollah.

Religious Divisions

Most of the Islamic world practices what is known as the Sunni branch of Islam. However, Iran asserts the Shia branch of the faith. There are substantial Shia minorities and even majorities in many countries. In Iraq, for example, the majority of the population is Shia. After the U.S. invasion of Iraq in 2003 Iran supported Shia terrorist groups in the country and helped to create a period of great instability. Iran also intervened to help President Assad in the Syrian Civil War.

Because it is Shia, the Iranian regime had poor relations with many radical Sunni terrorist groups, such as al-Qaeda. Iran is also seen as a rival to Saudi Arabia in the region, particularly in the states on the east side of the Arabian peninsula where there are substantial Shia minorities, and also in Yemen. Iran has been a serious source of volatility in the Middle East for decades.

2

3

KEY DATES

1979 Iranian Revolution is followed by Iraqi invasion of Iran and a war that lasts until August 1988.

1985 Hezbollah is founded in Lebanon with support from Iran.

2006 Iran gives aid to the Iraqi Shia militias known as the Mahdi army, led by Muqtada al-Sadr, during the Iraqi Civil War between Shia and Sunni groups.

November 23, 2015 Iran's Supreme Leader meets Vladimir Putin, president of Russia, in Tehran. It is believed they agree to coordinate support for President Assad's regime in the Syrian Civil War.

July 2018 Houthi rebels in Yemen attack a Saudi tanker. Iran helps to arm the Houthi who have been fighting a civil war since 2015 and are opposed by Saudi Arabia.

January 3, 2020 A U.S. air strike kills Iranian general Qasem Soleimani, head of the Iranian Revolutionary Guard and the Quds force, both of which had been active in Middle East terrorism.

4

5

1 Ayatollah Khomeini always followed a hard line, refusing to compromise with the Shah of Iran or, later, western governments.

2 A crowd holds up images of Muqtada al-Sadr after Iraqi election results in 2008 have gone in their direction.

3 The Ayatollah Khomeini walks down the steps of the aircraft that took him back to Iran in 1979 after a period of exile in France.

4 Muqtada al-Sadr headed a Shia group in Iraq and was given aid by the Iranian government.

5 Hassan Nasrallah, the leader of Hezbollah since the 1990s. He joined Hezbollah after the 1982 Israeli invasion of Lebanon.

Iraq

The invasion of Iraq and removal of its ruler, Saddam Hussein, was not an original aim of the "war on terror" but became crucial to its success.

↑ A U.S. soldier watches as a statue of Saddam Hussein is pulled down in central Baghdad in April 2003.

TIMELINE 2006 JULY–DECEMBER

KEY: Iraq | Afghanistan | International

July

July 11 India
Bombs on commuter trains in Mumbai kill 209 people and injure a further 714.

July 31 Afghanistan
NATO takes over military operations in the south of the country from the United States.

July 31 Germany
A planned terrorist attack on the German rail network fails.

August

August 10 Britain
British police foil a plot to blow up transatlantic airliners.

Operation Iraqi Freedom (OIF), the U.S.-led coalition's military operation in Iraq, began on March 20, 2003. The immediate goal, as argued by the Bush administration as a justification for going to war, was to remove Saddam Hussein's regime. The United States and its allies claimed it was necessary to destroy Saddam's ability to build or use weapons of mass destruction or to make them available to terrorists.

KEY DATES

March 20, 2003 A U.S.-led coalition begins the military invasion of Iraq.

December 14, 2003 Saddam Hussein is captured.

November 7–December 23, 2004 The Battle for Fallujah ends in a victory for U.S. forces.

December 15, 2005 Iraqis vote for the first full-term government since the invasion.

February 22, 2006 A bomb attack on a mosque in Samarra begins an upsurge in violence between Shias and Sunnis.

Continued on page 43

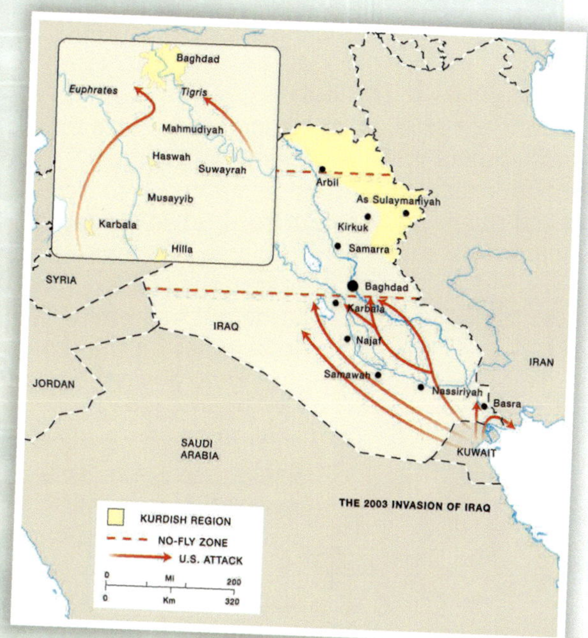

The invasion of Iraq was a short operation: It lasted less than a month.

December

October 5 Afghanistan
NATO takes control of military operations throughout the country.

November 23 Iraq
Car bombs and mortar attacks kill around 215 people in Sadr City, Baghdad.

December 6 United States
Nation-of-Islam convert Derrick Shareef is arrested during his plans to launch an attack on an Illinois shopping mall.

December 30 Iraq
Saddam Hussein is hanged.

Abu Ghraib

Abu Ghraib was a notorious prison near Baghdad where Saddam Hussein's secret police detained his enemies. After the invasion of Iraq, the prison was taken over by the U.S. military. In 2004, stories emerged of the ill-treatment of Iraqi detainees in the prison, and photographs showed U.S. personnel humiliating and taunting prisoners. The harsh treatment of the prisoners caused concern in the United States and great resentment in the Muslim world.

Rebuilding Iraq

After initial combat operations quickly drove Saddam from power, the focus of OIF shifted to the more open-ended mission of helping an emerging new Iraqi leadership. Over time, serious challenges to the Iraqi leadership grew from both homegrown insurgents and foreign fighters. The February 2006 bombing of the Golden Mosque in Samarra began a rise in religious violence, largely between Shia and Sunni Muslims. The character of the war changed from major battles to a counterinsurgency (COIN) and reconstruction effort.

Change of Direction

In January 2007, in an attempt to reverse the escalation of violence, President George W. Bush announced a fresh strategic approach to Iraq, called the "New Way Forward." The strategy included a "surge" of additional U.S. forces being sent to the country. The surge put into effect COIN approaches on the ground that were designed to promote population security, such as troops living among the local population at small outposts. Over the course of the surge, security conditions on the ground

➔ A U.S. military policeman arrests a former Iraqi soldier.

TIMELINE 2007 JANUARY-JUNE

KEY: Iraq | Afghanistan | International

January

January 10 Iraq
President George W. Bush announces a new strategy involving a "surge" of thousands more U.S. troops in Iraq.

March

March 16 Afghanistan
NATO forces launch Operation Achilles against the Taliban in the south of the country.

March 27 Iraq
Shia pilgrims are targeted by truck bombs at Tal Afar; 152 pilgrims die.

← Murals in Iran illustrate scenes of U.S. mistreatment of prisoners in Abu Ghraib.

improved. In August 2008, the outgoing commander of Multinational Force–Iraq, U.S. General David Petraeus, agreed that the surge had made "significant progress." However, he argued that progress toward peace and stability in Iraq was "still not self-sustaining."

The Iraqis Take Power

As Iraqi capabilities grew, Iraqi officials became more assertive and less inclined to consult with U.S. advisors. The Iraqi government wanted to speed up its assumption of full responsibility for Iraq. In February 2009, President Barack Obama announced that the last U.S. combat troops would leave Iraq the following year; the last brigade withdrew on August 19, 2010. However, some 50,000 U.S. troops remained in Iraq in an "advisory capacity" to help train Iraqi forces. Further, the United States announced that from 2011 it would also take charge of training the Iraqi police force.

Continued from page 41

December 30, 2006 Saddam Hussein is executed.

January 10, 2007 President Bush announces troop surge.

March 25–31, 2008 Iraqi forces reclaim much of Basra from militia control.

January 1, 2009 Iraq takes control of security in Baghdad's Green Zone.

February 27, 2009 President Obama announces withdrawal of U.S. troops by next year.

October 25, 2009 Two car bombs kill at least 155 people, the deadliest attacks since April 2007.

August 19, 2010 The last U.S. combat troops leave Iraq.

April 18 Iraq
Some 130 people die in a suicide attack on Sadriya market in Baghdad, the largest single attack for years.

May

May 12 Afghanistan
The senior Taliban commander, Mullah Dadullah, is killed fighting U.S. forces.

June 30 Britain
Islamists launch an unsuccessful attack on Glasgow airport.

IN FOCUS

ISIS

The eruption of ISIS onto the world stage in 2014 brought new instability to Iraq.

1

One of the most unwelcome by-products of the religious and political internal warfare in Iraq after 2010 was the emergence of the group known as Islamic State or ISIS. This had been formed in 1999, originally paying allegiance to al-Qaeda. It built up its strength in Iraq, and then in 2014 proclaimed itself a worldwide caliphate. It launched effective propaganda campaigns among Muslims throughout the world, and recruits flocked to it. Young men and women from Europe, for example, ran away from home to join ISIS.

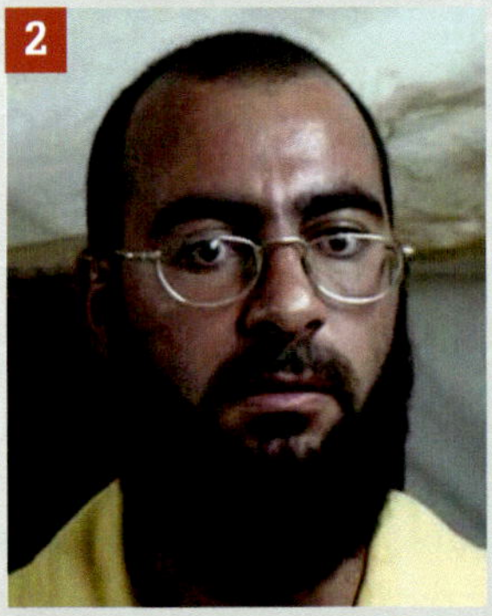

2

Persecuting Minorities

During the period 2014 to 2016 ISIS took over large parts of Iraq and Syria, ruling an area containing about 10 million people and the major city of Mosul. In this region ISIS persecuted religious minorities such as Christians and Yazidis and Shia Muslims. A coalition of forces eventually contained and then defeated ISIS. This coalition included Kurdish troops as well as U.S. and Iraqi units.

Although its territorial ambitions had been reversed, ISIS remained a powerful force. Its members were also active in Afghanistan.

3

4

5

6

KEY DATES

1999 ISIS is formed by Abu Musab al-Zarqawi. It is also known as Islamic State, or sometimes Daesh, its Arabic-language acronym.

June 2014 ISIS takes over Anbar province in Iraq, defeating government forces there.

June 10, 2014 ISIS takes the city of Mosul. The group is estimated to have killed 4,000 Iraqi government troops that had surrendered.

May 2015 ISIS controls its maximum territory in Syria and Iraq. Young Muslims from Europe evade detection and fly to the Middle East in order to join ISIS.

July 2017 Mosul is retaken after a general offensive by Kurdish, Iraqi, and Syrian forces.

1 An early ISIS attack: the result of the bombing of the office of the U.N. Humanitarian Coordinator in Iraq.

2 Abu Bakr al-Baghdadi, leader of ISIS from 2014 to 2019. He was killed in a surprise raid by U.S. special forces in October 2019.

3 The destruction of whole areas of the Syrian city of Raqqa was a result of the fighting when government forces moved against ISIS to liberate the city.

4 The Temple of Bel at Palmyra. ISIS refused to recognize the value of ancient civilizations and destroyed such buildings.

5 The flag used by ISIS. The appeal of ISIS to young people across the world surprised many in the west.

6 Kurdish Peshmerga forces in northern Iraq. The Kurds played an important part in the defeat of ISIS in Iraq.

The Middle East

From 2001, the United States launched major initiatives across the region to remake the Middle East as part of its efforts to stop Islamic extremism from taking hold.

↑ A Lebanese woman shows her support for Hezbollah, a Shia group blamed for terror attacks in Israel.

TIMELINE 2007 JULY–DECEMBER

KEY: Iraq | Afghanistan | International

July

August Afghanistan
NATO reports that illegal opium production is at a record high.

August 25 India
Twin bombs detonate in Hyderabad, killing 44.

August 14 Iraq
Bombs in the northern city of Qahtanlya kill more than 500 people.

September

September 4 Europe
Police arrest suspected Islamist terrorists in Germany and Denmark.

Poster for al-Qaeda suspects in Saudi Arabia and Yemen.

The United States aimed to transform a region that had sunk into economic stagnation, religious turmoil, and conflict. Al-Qaeda and other Islamist groups continued to draw support across the region. In part, their popularity reflects continuing resentment of the creation of Israel in 1948 on Arab-occupied land and of the Israeli treatment of the Palestinians.

Saudi Arabia

Saudi Arabia is one of the major regional powers and home to the most important Muslim holy sites. It has two opposing political groups: modernists on the one hand and traditionalist Wahhabi clerics on the other. With half of all Saudis under the age of 20, and demanding economic development, the conservative clerics, who own many state institutions such as schools, face a considerable challenge.

KEY DATES

June 24, 2002 President George W. Bush outlines a "road map" for peace that calls for an independent Palestinian state coexisting with Israel.

May 12, 2003 At least 35 people are killed in suicide attacks on Western compounds in the Saudi city of Riyadh.

December 12, 2003 President Bush signs the Syrian Accountability Act, which imposes trade and financial sanctions as punishment for Syria's support of terrorism.

December 6, 2004 Militants storm the U.S. Consulate in Jeddah, Saudia Arabia, killing seven people.

August 15, 2005 Israel begins to pull out of the Gaza Strip.

November 9, 2005 Coordinated bomb attacks on hotels in Amman, Jordan, kill at least 60 people.

Continued on page 49

October 18 Pakistan
Hours after her return to the country from exile, former president Benazir Bhutto survives bomb attacks that kill 136 of her followers.

November Pakistan
The Pakistan military intensifies actions against Islamic militants in the Swat Valley.

December

December 16 Iraq
U.K. forces hand control of the southern city of Basra to Iraqi forces.

December 27 Pakistan
Benazir Bhutto is shot dead by an assassin who then blows himself up.

Hamas

Hamas was founded in 1987 as an Islamist group that aimed to drive Israel from what it saw as Palestinian land. There was a tradition of terror attacks in the region, and Hamas's military brigade was notorious for carrying out suicide bombing raids within Israel. In 2006, Hamas won a majority in Palestinian elections and effectively took charge of Gaza.

The Road Map

The Arab-Israeli issue continues to dominate the region. A U.S.-led "road map" that would lead to lasting peace failed. Despite an Israeli withdrawal from the Gaza Strip in late 2003, the Israelis continued to build settlements on occupied land in the West Bank. Meanwhile, Palestinian terrorists continued to kill dozens of Israeli citizens, often in suicide attacks.

The "War on Terror"

After the terrorist attacks of 9/11, 2001, Arab countries led by Syria, Egypt, and Jordan condemned the attacks and offered the United States assistance. However, in September 2002,

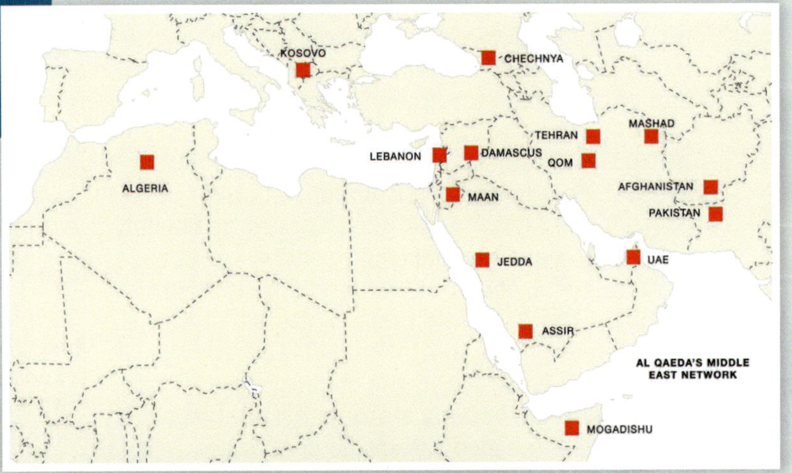

→ The main al-Qaeda bases in the Middle East. Each base can act on its own or in cooperation with others.

TIMELINE 2008 JANUARY–JUNE

KEY: Iraq | Afghanistan | International

January 13 Iraq
Members of Saddam Hussein's Baath Party are allowed to hold formal office again.

January

March

March 28 Iraq
Iraqi forces launch a crackdown on the city of Basra, where they fight the Mehdi Army of Moqtada al-Sadr.

In 2006, Israel blockaded Lebanon to prevent supplies reaching Hezbollah.

when U.S. President Bush sought U.N. consent to invade Iraq as part of the "war on terror," all three countries voted against the invasion. Once the Iraq war began, they suffered economically, as they depended on Iraq for oil and trade. Arab leaders were torn between stability and reform. Jordan introduced a form of parliamentary government, but Syria largely ignored its commitments to the United States' effort and continued to support terrorist groups.

Continued from page 47

January 26, 2006 The Islamist Hamas party wins Palestinian elections in Gaza.

June 28–November 26, 2006 The Second Intifada, or uprising, sees fighting between Israel and Palestine in the Gaza Strip.

July 12–August 14, 2006 War in Lebanon sees the Israelis claim victory over the Islamist Hezbollah movement.

May 20–September 7, 2007 A battle between the Islamist Fatah al-Islam party and the Lebanese army ends in victory for the army.

December 27, 2008–January 18, 2009 Israel attacks the Gaza Strip, and Hamas suffers heavy losses.

August 28, 2009 A suicide bomber blows himself up at a party in Jeddah attended by Prince Mohammed bin Nayef, head of Saudi security.

An Israeli soldier fires tear gas at Palestinian protestors in the West Bank.

May

June

May 18 India
The city of Jaipur is rocked by eight simultaneous bombs that kill 63 people.

June 14 Afghanistan
In a jailbreak in Kandahar, more than 350 Taliban prisoners escape.

June 17 Iraq
A Shia market is bombed in Baghdad, killing some 63 people.

Arab Spring and Syrian War

The Arab Spring proved to be a false dawn for the spread of democracy in the Middle East.

After the invasions of Afghanistan and Iraq the examples of free elections in both countries acted as something of a catalyst for those in the Arab world that had been wanting to establish democracy. Starting in Tunisia in 2010, there was a wave of revolution in the Arab world that was sometimes called the Arab Spring. Old governments were forced out and new ones came in. However, these movements for democracy were mostly short-lived. In Egypt, for example, Mohamed Morsi was elected president but in a year had been ousted by a coup.

1

2

Syria

Syria's ruler, Bashar al-Assad, was almost forced out by a popular uprising in 2011, but managed to survive with help from Iran and army support. Western powers did not intervene and Russia stepped into the vacuum, supplying Assad with arms. Turkey also stepped in. Millions became refugees as the war destabilized the whole region. By 2022, the rebels were reduced to holding out in a few enclaves and Syria was in ruins.

3

4

5

6

KEY DATES

2010 Protests in Tunisia against the repressive regime lead to similar protests across the Arab world.

2011 Egyptian dictator Hosni Mubarak is toppled by widespread demonstrations. Mohamed Morsi is elected president, but ousted in a military coup a year later.

August 20, 2014 A U.N. survey concludes that at least 191,369 people had died in the Syrian Civil War to date.

September 2015 Russia sends aid to the Assad regime, and begins a campaign of air strikes against opposition enclaves.

October 2019 Turkey invades northern Syria to establish a 20-mile (30 km) "safe zone" in which it intends to resettle refugees. This is widely seen as an attack on Kurdish nationalists holding the area.

2022 It is estimated that 5.6 million refugees have fled the fighting in Syria. Over 3.7 million are in Turkey.

1 A Syrian rebel, part of the so-called "Army of Glory," launches a wire-guided missile against Syrian government positions.

2 Mass demonstration in Tahrir Square, Cairo, in February 2011 that led to the downfall of Egyptian dictator Hosni Mubarak.

3 A Russian Sukhoi Su-34 at Latakia airport in Syria as Russia sends in weapons and personnel to help the Syrian government.

4 Street protests spread across the Arab world in 2010 and 2011. Young people tried to make a stand for democracy.

5 Syrians demonstrate in 2011. At first, the regime seemed about to topple, but the army supported Bashar al-Assad.

6 Syrian President Assad meets Russian leader Vladimir Putin in 2020. Russian intervention turned the tide in Assad's favor.

Southeast Asia

Many terrorist groups that operate across Southeast Asia are not well known. Despite having different goals, most of them cooperate freely with each other.

↑ An Indonesian wears a shirt bearing an image of Osama bin Laden. Some Indonesian Muslims see bin Laden as an Islamic hero.

TIMELINE 2008 JULY–DECEMBER

KEY: Iraq | Afghanistan | International

July

July 7 Afghanistan
Pakistan is blamed for a suicide attack on the Indian Embassy in Kabul that kills 50 people.

August Pakistan
Another intense campaign against militants begins in the Swat Valley.

September

September 9 United States
President George W. Bush announces sending 4,500 more U.S. troops to Afghanistan in what is called a "quiet surge."

September 20 Pakistan
A car bomb at the popular Marriott hotel in Islamabad kills more than 60 and leaves 250 injured.

Southeast Asia has numerous different kinds of terrorist organizations, many of which are motivated by a fundamentalist interpretation of Islam. These organizations are characterized by high degrees of cooperation. Even insurgent groups that do not share the same goals cooperate across national boundaries. That allows them jointly to develop logistics and training, and to establish safe havens. For example, Jemaah Islamiyah, which is based in Indonesia and traditionally has very strong ties with al-Qaeda, has operated in the Philippines. Abu Sayyaf, which means "bearer of the sword" in Arabic, is a militant group based in the southern Philippines that seeks to create a separate Islamic state for the country's Muslim minority. The U.S. government condemns Abu Sayyaf as a terrorist group linked to Osama bin Laden's al-Qaeda network.

Intelligence Failures

Recent events in the war on terrorism have made Southeast Asia central to the U.S. strategy to defeat

KEY DATES

October 12, 2002 Bombs in nightclubs on Bali, Indonesia, kill 202 people. Jemaah Islamiyah is blamed; the United States lists it as a terrorist organization.

August 5, 2003 A car bomb at the Marriott Hotel in Jakarta, Indonesia, kills 12 people.

August 12, 2003 Riduan Isamuddin, known as Hambali, the suspected planner of the Bali bombings, is captured.

September 9, 2004 A bomb attack on the Australian Embassy in Jakarta.

October 1, 2005 Suicide bombers hit tourist area of Bali, killing 20 people and injuring more than 130.

August 12, 2007 In Jakarta, the Islamist Hizb ut-Tahrir group calls for the creation of a single caliphate across the Muslim world.

Continued on page 55

Police in Indonesia stand guard at the trial of an alleged terrorist.

November 16 Iraq
The Iraqi Parliament approves a security pact with the United States under which all U.S. troops will leave Iraq by the end of 2011.

November 26–29 India
Gunmen launch attacks on eight sites in Mumbai, including railroad stations and tourist hotels; there are 173 confirmed dead. The attackers are thought to be sponsored by Pakistan.

December Pakistan
Press reports claim that Islamic militants now control 75 percent of the Swat Valley.

The Bali Bombs

On October 12, 2002, three explosions rocked the resort of Kuta on the island of Bali in Indonesia. The main targets were popular nightclubs. A total of 202 people died, with 240 injured; of the dead, 38 were Indonesians and 88 were Australian tourists. The attacks were the most deadly episode in the struggle by extremists to establish an Islamic state in Southeast Asia. The group Jemaah Islamiyah was blamed. Three of its members were executed for the crime in 2008.

➔ A leader of the Moro Islamic Liberation Front is arrested in the Philippines.

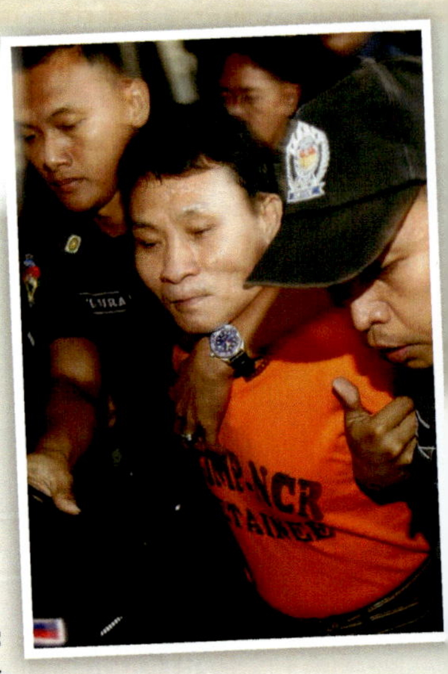

terrorism. However, many of Southeast Asia's terrorist groups are not on the U.S. State Department's list of Foreign Terrorist Organizations (FTO). This means that current policies attack only a portion of the broader terrorist network. In addition, although terrorists in Southeast Asia work closely together, their governments often do not. The terrorists take advantage of this poor regional cooperation to hide from the authorities by moving to the country next door.

➔ A U.S. airman shows his Filipino counterparts how to use emergency equipment.

Government Weakness

Terrorist groups have sought refuge where local authorities are least committed to countering terrorism, notably in Indonesia and the Philippines.

TIMELINE 2009 JANUARY–JUNE

KEY: Iraq | Afghanistan | International

January

March

January 24 Somalia
A car bomb kills 16 people in the Somali capital, Mogadishu.

February 17 Afghanistan
The United States announces it will send a further 17,000 troops to Afghanistan; other NATO countries also increase their commitment to the country.

March 3 Pakistan
Gunmen hold up a minibus carrying members of the Sri Lankan cricket team, causing widespread shock in the cricket-loving subcontinent.

The Philippine government may be the weakest link in Southeast Asia's antiterrorist efforts. There have been few terrorist arrests in the Philippines. The existence of a safe haven in Mindanao in the southern Philippines permits Southeast Asia's terrorist brotherhood to plan and train. However, in 2009 and 2010, government forces again achieved some minor but promising victories against both Abu Sayyaf and Jemaah Islamiyah. The same period saw the Indonesian government make some significant breakthroughs.

Continued from page 53

November 9, 2008
Three members of Jemaah Islamiyah are executed for 2002 Bali bombings.

July 17, 2009
Two suicide bombs in Marriott and Ritz-Carlton hotels in Jakarta kill nine people.

September 17, 2009
Indonesian police shoot dead the country's most-wanted Islamist militant, Noordin Mohammad Top.

September 21, 2009
The Philippine army captures a commander of the Moro Islamic Liberation Front.

March 10, 2010 The mastermind of the Bali bombings, Dulmatin, is confirmed dead.

Indonesian police walk past wreckage after the Bali bombing of 2002.

March 27 United States
President Barack Obama announces a new strategy including sending a further 4,000 personnel to Afghanistan.

June

June 10 Afghanistan
General Stanley McChrystal takes over as commander of U.S. forces as part of an attempt to break the deadlock.

June 30 Iraq
Iraqis celebrate their "day of sovereignty" as U.S. troops withdraw from Iraq towns and cities.

The United States

While the U.S. public grew increasingly skeptical about the wars in Iraq and Afghanistan, the fear of homegrown terrorist attacks continued.

➔ A watchtower guards the fence at the prison camp at Guantanamo Bay in Cuba.

TIMELINE 2009 JULY–DECEMBER

KEY: Iraq | Afghanistan | International

July

July 2 Afghanistan
U.S. troops launch a massive offensive against the Taliban in southern Helmand province.

August United States
President Obama announces that all U.S. troops will leave Iraq by August 2010.

September

September 17 Somalia
Terrorists bomb the African Union base at Mogadishu.

Two F-16s fly over San Francisco in a training exercise.

In December 2001, 92 percent of Americans told pollsters that they were satisfied with U.S. progress in the "war on terror." Ten years later, in January 2011, after the invasion of and withdrawal from Iraq, that figure had fallen to 39 percent.

Negative Perceptions

The decline in the war's popularity had many causes, including a series of scandals. In 2004, photographs emerged of U.S. personnel mistreating Iraqi detainees in the prison at Abu Ghraib. The Central Intelligence Agency was accused of torturing suspected terrorists. Many Americans were troubled by the detention of prisoners at a U.S. base in Guantanamo Bay, Cuba. The prisoners were classed as "enemy combatants" and held in harsh conditions, without trial. After Barack Obama became

KEY DATES

October 7, 2001 President Bush announces Operation Enduring Freedom, which will send troops to Afghanistan to fight the Taliban.

October 26, 2001 President Bush signs the Patriot Act, which gives authorities wide powers to fight terrorism.

December 22, 2001 Richard Reid, a British national, tries to detonate a bomb hidden in his shoe on a Miami-bound flight.

January 11, 2002 Prisoners arrive at Guantanamo Bay, Cuba.

November 25, 2002 President Bush signs the Homeland Security Act into law.

March 20, 2003 U.S. troops lead the invasion of Iraq.

April 28, 2004 The popular CBS *60 Minutes* show reports on alleged abuse at the Abu Ghraib prison in Baghdad by U.S. military personnel.

Continued on page 59

November

November 2 Afghanistan Hamid Kharzai's reelection as president is confirmed.

November 5 United States A Muslim U.S. Army major, Nidal Malik Hasan, shoots dead 13 people at Fort Hood in Texas; 30 people are wounded.

December

December 1 United States Barack Obama announces a further 30,000 U.S. troops will be sent to Afghanistan, raising the total to 100,000.

December Iraq A group linked to al-Qaeda is blamed for a wave of suicide bombs in Baghdad.

December 25 United States A Nigerian attempts to blow up an airliner flying from Paris to Detroit; his bomb only sets fire to his underwear.

The PATRIOT Act

Passed in October 2001, the USA PATRIOT Act aimed to improve the ability of security services to prevent terrorism. The act improved communications between agencies, for example. It also increased official powers to monitor both immigrants and citizens, including by reading their mail or listening to phone calls. Many people protested that such powers were a breach of civil liberties.

president in January 2009, he announced plans to transfer prisoners to the mainland.

Falling Optimism

The decline in the war's popularity also reflected growing U.S. casualties. Some 4,301 American service personnel died in Iraq, and more than 31,000 had been injured; in Afghanistan, as troop numbers increased in 2009, some 714 had died. As the cost of the war rose, optimism fell. In May 2003, George W. Bush announced that the military struggle in Iraq had been won.

But despite more than 160,000 U.S. troops in the country, terrorists continued to strike. Iraqi civilians died in high numbers, while the government was unable to establish strong governance. The Taliban proved a difficult enemy in Afghanistan, too.

➔ An expert examines the car bomb found in Times Square in 2010.

TIMELINE 2010 JANUARY-DECEMBER

KEY: Iraq | Afghanistan | International

January — March

February 13 Afghanistan
NATO forces launch Operation Moshtarak in southern Helmand province.

March 29 Russia
Two female suicide bombers kill 40 people and injure more than 100 on the Moscow metro system.

May 1 United States
A car bomb is spotted and defused in Times Square, New York City.

→ U.S. demonstrators protest against the PATRIOT Act of 2001.

Even after the U.S. withdrew from Iraq in 2010, some Americans worried that the "war on terror" could not be won.

Homegrown Plots

At home, the PATRIOT Act of 2001 remained controversial, but plots by American Islamists failed or were thwarted. They included an attempt to detonate a car bomb in Times Square, New York City, in May 2010; the bomb was defused after it was spotted by police.

↓ Continued from page 57

January 20, 2009 Barack Obama is sworn in as the 44th president of the United States.

January 22, 2009 President Obama orders the closure of Guantanamo Bay.

November 5, 2009 U.S. Army major Nidal Malik Hasan, a Muslim, shoots dead 13 people at Fort Hood, Texas.

December 25, 2009 A Nigerian attempts to blow up a Detroit-bound flight.

May 1, 2010 A car bomb is diffused in Times Square, New York, with no casualties.

August 19, 2010 The last U.S. troops leave Iraq.

May 1, 2011 U.S. special forces kill Osama bin Laden during a raid in Abbottabad, Pakistan.

← Lines at airports are a visible sign of increased security.

April 23 Iraq A wave of bombings kills 85 people in Baghdad.

July

July 20 Afghanistan An international conference endorses President Karzai's plan for the future security of the country.

August 19 Iraq The last U.S. combat brigade leaves Iraq seven years after the invasion.

September 29 Europe Police thwart planned gun and bomb attacks in France, Britain, and Germany.

December

December 11 Sweden Two car bombs in the center of Stockholm kill an Islamist bomber and injure two people.

IN FOCUS

Aftermath of the War on Terror

The War on Terror spilled over into many areas of the world but there was no definite conclusion to the conflict.

The War on Terror undertaken during the presidency of George W. Bush led to the invasion of two nations, Afghanistan and Iraq, and to regime change in both of them. However, these open-ended commitments proved troubling. U.S. troops were engaged for long periods in support of governments that were corrupt and sometimes incompetent. As with many wars, there were surprising twists and turns after the initial successes. In Iraq, for example, the descent into bloody sectarian and religious violence led to the growth of the terrorist group ISIS that at one stage threatened to take over the country and remained influential over much of the Middle East and Africa into the 2020s.

Refugee Crisis

The example of Iraq led the West to be very wary of intervening elsewhere, as was demonstrated when opportunities to intervene in the Syrian Civil War were not taken. A wave of refugees fled the country, Russia entered the war on behalf of the government of Bashar al-Assad, and the ramifications were felt in all neighboring states.

The "war on terror" certainly lessened the threat from al-Qaeda, and Osama bin Laden was killed. However, the world had become, perhaps, an even more dangerous place in the following decade.

KEY DATES

2011 U.S. forces officially leave Iraq.

2011 Osama bin Laden killed in Pakistan.

2014 U.S. forces return to Iraq.

2015 Terrorist group ISIS controls large parts of Iraq and Syria before being defeated in 2017.

January 2015 NATO forces officially ended their combat role in Afghanistan in December 2014. Now, in Operation Resolute Support, they take on the role of training the Afghan national army in its fight against the Taliban.

August 2021 U.S. evacuation of Kabul. Taliban return to power in Afghanistan.

1 Thankful Afghans cram into the hold of a C-17 as they are evacuated from Afghanistan after the Taliban takeover of 2021.

2 Troops pull a young boy into a truck as the evacuation of civilians from Afghanistan gathers pace.

3 One of the huge refugee camps built in Turkey to house the millions of people who fled there from the Syrian Civil War.

4 Daily life in Kabul changed in 2021 as groups of armed Taliban fighters took over the streets of the city.

5 The final American soldier to leave Afghanistan, Major General Christopher Donahue, photographed with a night-vision camera as he walks up the aircraft ramp.

Glossary

alliance An agreement between countries to cooperate.

arms embargo A ban on selling or transporting arms to a particular government or country.

caliphate A spiritual Islamic government ruled by a caliph; some Muslims want to establish a caliphate that stretches across many countries.

coalition The temporary uniting of different forces, such as countries or political parties.

drone An unmanned aircraft that is guided by remote control.

extremism A belief in an extreme version of views or opinions.

fundamentalist Someone who believes in a very simple, black-and-white form of a religion.

governance The act of governing a country.

hijack To seize an airplane or other means of transportation and force it to go to a particular destination.

intelligence Information about the intentions or operations of an enemy.

intifada A Palestinian uprising against the Israeli government.

Islamist A Muslim who believes that society should be organized according to the laws of Islam.

militia Unofficial citizen army.

Muslim A follower of Islam.

nationalist Someone who believes that his or her nation and its interests are more important than all others.

radical Someone who holds extreme political or religious views.

safe haven A place where an individual or group is protected by the government.

separatists People who want to separate a particular region from a country, either to become independent or to become part of another country.

Shia A Muslim who follows a minority version of Islam that is particularly strong in Iran.

suicide bomber Someone who carries out a bombing attack during which he or she will also be killed by the bomb.

Sunni A Muslim who follows the majority version of Islam.

terrorist Someone who tries to achieve political goals by using random acts of violence to cause widespread fear.

Further Resources

Books

Adams, Simon. *The Iraq War (Secret History)*. Arcturus Publishing, 2011.

Bailey, Diane. *Rescue from an ISIS Prison! Delta Force in Iraq during the War on Terror*. Mason Crest, 2019.

Crawford, Steve. *War on Terror* (Facts at Your Fingertips). Brown Bear Books, 2010.

Gerber, Larry. *The Taliban in Afghanistan*. Rosen Classroom, 2010.

Lawrence, Blythe. *War and Terrorism in the Twenty-First Century*. ReferencePoint Press, 2020.

Miller, Mara. *Remembering September 11, 2001: What We Know Now*. Enslow Publishers, 2011.

Romero, Libby. *September 11*. National Geographic Kids, 2021.

Rusick, Jessica. *The War on Terror: Then and Now*. Abdo & Daughters, 2021.

Thiel, Kristin. *True Teen Stories* from Syria: Surviving Civil War. Cavendish Square, 2019.

Williams, Brian. *The War on Terror* (Secret History). Arcturus Publishing, 2011.

Websites

news.bbc.co.uk/1/hi/in_depth/world/2001/war_on_terror
BBC news site special report on Investigating al-Qaeda.

www.globalissues.org/issue/245/war-on-terror
Edition of Global Issues that focuses on the war on terror.

www.september11news.com/
An in-depth archive of world reaction to the terrorist attacks of 9/11, 2001.

www.globalsecurity.org/military/ops/enduring-freedom.htm
Global Security page with links to historical and ongoing aspects of Operation Enduring Freedom.

history.army.mil/books/wot_artwork/wot_artbook.html
Army artists looking at the war on terrorism, 2001 to present.

Index